Roy.T.Lewis

BUSINESS

Success Blueprint 2023/2024

By Roy.T.Lewis

DESCRIPTION

In "The Business Success Blueprint," author ROY. T

.LEWIS presents a comprehensive guide to achieving success in the business world. Drawing on his extensive experience as a successful entrepreneur, ROY shares practical advice and actionable tips to help aspiring and existing business owners navigate the complexities of today's competitive landscape. Whether you're just starting out or looking to take your business to the next level, this book offers valuable insights and strategies for achieving sustained success.

TABLE OF CONTENTS

- The importance of a clear vision and purpose for your business

- Setting ambitious yet achievable goals

- Aligning your values with your business objectives

- Developing a compelling mission statement

Chapter 2: Building a Strong Foundation

- Understanding your target market and customer needs

- Conducting thorough market research and analysis

- Crafting a unique value proposition

- Establishing a solid business plan and strategy

Chapter 3: Effective Leadership and Team Building

- The role of leadership in driving business success

- Cultivating a positive and motivating work environment

- Hiring the right people and building a high-performing team

- Developing strong communication and collaboration skills

Chapter 4: Customer-Centric Approach

- Putting customers at the center of your business

- Creating exceptional customer experiences

- Building customer loyalty and advocacy

- Harnessing the power of feedback and continuous improvement

Chapter 5: Marketing and Branding Strategies

- Developing a strong brand identity and positioning

- Implementing effective marketing strategies for maximum reach

- Leveraging digital marketing channels and social media

- Measuring marketing effectiveness and adjusting strategies

Chapter 6: Sales and Revenue Growth

- Building a robust sales pipeline

- Effective sales techniques and negotiation skills

- Developing strategic partnerships and collaborations

- Maximizing revenue growth through innovation and diversification

Chapter 7: Financial Management and Profitability

- Essential financial management practices for business success

- Budgeting, forecasting, and financial analysis

- Managing cash flow and working capital

importance to society.

- Acknowledging the challenges and need for effective solutions.

- Setting the objectives for revitalizing the economy.

Chapter 12: Understanding Economic Systems

- Overview of different economic systems (capitalism, socialism, mixed economies).

- Analyzing the strengths and weaknesses of each system.

- Assessing the current economic system and identifying areas for improvement.

Chapter 13: Identifying Key Economic Issues

- Examining the root causes of economic problems (unemployment, inflation, income inequality, etc.).

- Understanding the interdependencies among different issues.

- Prioritizing the most pressing economic issues to address.

Chapter 14: Fiscal Policy and Government Intervention

- Exploring the role of fiscal policy in economic stability and growth.

- Evaluating the effectiveness of government intervention.

- Strategies for using fiscal policy to stimulate economic growth, reduce unemployment, and control inflation.

Chapter 15: Monetary Policy and Central Banking

- Understanding the functions of central banks in managing the economy.

- Analyzing the tools and techniques of monetary policy.

- Discussing the relationship between interest rates, money supply, and economic performance.

Chapter 16: Encouraging Innovation and Entrepreneurship

- Highlighting the role of innovation in driving economic growth.

- Identifying barriers to innovation and entrepreneurship.

- Strategies to promote a culture of innovation, support startups, and foster entrepreneurship.

Chapter 17: Investing in Human Capital

- Recognizing the importance of education and skills development.

- Enhancing access to quality education and vocational training.

- Addressing the skills gap and promoting lifelong learning.

Chapter 18: International Trade and Economic Integration

- Examining the benefits and challenges of international trade.

- Analyzing trade agreements and their impact on the economy.

- Strategies for expanding international trade and attracting foreign investment.

Chapter 19: Sustainable Development and Green Economy

- Understanding the concept of sustainable development.

- Exploring the potential of green technologies and renewable energy.

- Promoting environmentally friendly practices and transitioning to a green economy.

Chapter 20: Strengthening Infrastructure and Public

Investment

- Assessing the importance of infrastructure for economic development.

- Strategies for financing and implementing infrastructure projects.

- Maximizing the impact of public investment on economic growth.

Chapter 21: Social Welfare and Inclusive Growth

- Addressing income inequality and social disparities.

- Implementing policies to promote inclusive growth.

- Ensuring social safety nets and support for vulnerable populations.

MOST POPULAR BUSINESSES

23. E -commerce and online retail selling:

- "Electronic transactions: the strategy of launching and scaling the successful online stores"

- "Digital marketing technology: stimulation of traffic sales and growth"

- "Control of the experience of consumers: it creates loyalty in the digital age"

- "Optimization of the delivery chain: simplifying the adaptation to the success of electronic trade"

- "World range of quantitative age: the opportunity of online retailers"

24. Consultancy and professional services:

- "Trust counselor: they form relationships with customers and winners".

- "Research tips: tools, equipment and tools to achieve success."

- "Effective communication technology: customer, reliable and influence"

- "Strategic consultation: Development and implementation of business"

- "Consulting Business Model Management: Management Project"

25. The food and drink industry:

- "Achievements of the restaurant: opening more than concepts"

- "Hobers Entrepreneuriat: Commission and maintenance of the food company"

- "Engineering menu: menu by strategic design"

- "Farmer table: permanent experience in the food industry"

CONCLUSION

CHAPTER 1

A clear vision and purpose for your business is critical to long-term success and growth. A well-defined vision provides direction and guidance to help you make strategic decisions and set meaningful goals. Some key points to consider are:

1. **The Importance of a Clear Vision and Purpose:** A clear vision reflects the desired future state of the company. This includes your ambitions, the impact you want to have and the values that guide your actions. A well-crafted vision statement inspires and motivates both the team and stakeholders, creates a shared sense of purpose, and drives everyone toward a common goal.

2. **Set Ambitious But Achievable Goals:** Having a clear vision is very important to set ambitious and achievable goals. Ambitious goals encourage you to strive for excellence, think creatively and step out of your comfort zone. However, it is important to ensure

that these goals are realistic and achievable within a specific time frame. Set measurable milestones along the way so you can monitor your progress and make necessary adjustments.

3. **Align your values with your business goals:** Your values must closely align with your business goals. When your values align with your goals, you create wholeness and authenticity. These alignments help build trust with customers, employees and other stakeholders. By integrating our values into our decision-making process, we ensure that our business activities are aligned with our core beliefs.

4. **Essential Mission Statement Development:** A

mission statement succinctly describes the company's purpose, core activities, and the value it provides to its customers. You should explain what makes your company different from other companies and why it is important to you. A well-crafted mission statement can be a powerful tool to recruit and attract customers and differentiate your company in a competitive market.

Define your vision by engaging key stakeholders, including employees, customers and partners. Gather insights, ideas and perspectives to create a vision that everyone involved can relate to. We regularly review and revise our vision statement to ensure it remains relevant as the business evolves.

Remember, a strong vision and purpose is the basis for strategic planning, goal setting and decision making. By aligning your values with your goals and articulating your mission, you inspire your team, engage your customers, and ultimately achieve long-term success.

CHAPTER 2

Building a solid business foundation requires several important steps and considerations. The four key elements to focus on are:

1. Understand your target market and customer needs:

Before starting a business, it is very important to have a good understanding of your target market and the needs of your potential customers. This includes researching your target audience's demographics, behaviors, preferences and pain points. By understanding their needs, you can develop products or services that effectively solve their problems or satisfy their needs.

2. Conduct thorough market research and analysis:

Market research helps us understand the industry environment, competition, trends and consumer behavior. This involves analyzing data and information to identify opportunities and potential barriers. In-depth market research enables you to make informed decisions about pricing, positioning, marketing strategy and product/service development.

3. Create a unique value proposition:

A value proposition is a clear statement that describes the unique benefits customers will receive if they choose you over your competitors. You need to clearly communicate the value your products and services provide and how they meet the needs of your target market. A compelling value proposition can help differentiate your business and attract customers.

4. Establish a clear business plan and strategy:

A well-designed business plan is essential to managing your business and securing investment or funding. It explains business objectives, target markets, competitive analysis, marketing and sales strategies, financial forecasts and operational details. A strong strategy includes actionable steps to achieve business goals and provides a road map to success.

In addition, there are other aspects that contribute to building a solid foundation, such as:

- Develop a strong brand identity and positioning that resonates with your target audience. - Build a talented and dedicated team that aligns with your business goals. - Implement effective marketing and promotion strategies to reach and captivate your target audience.

- Build strong relationships with suppliers, partners and stakeholders. - Establish reliable systems and processes for efficient operation and customer satisfaction.

- Regularly review and adjust strategies based on market dynamics and customer feedback.

Remember, building a strong foundation requires constant effort and adaptation. Being flexible and responsive to market changes and customer needs is essential to ensure the long-term success of your business.

CHAPTER 3

Effective leadership and team building are essential components of business success. Here are some key points to consider for each topic.

1. The role of leadership in entrepreneurial success:

- Vision and Strategy: Leaders must have a clear vision and create a strategic plan to drive the organization toward its goals.

- Decision making: Effective leaders make informed decisions, consider the views of various stakeholders and analyze possible outcomes.

- Inspiration and motivation: Leaders inspire their teams by setting a positive example, motivating them to do their best and instilling a sense of purpose. -

Adaptability: Leaders must be flexible and adaptable to

change, identify opportunities and lead teams through challenges. - Accountability: Strong leaders take responsibility for their actions and the results of their teams, foster a culture of accountability, and continuously improve.

2. Creating a positive and motivating work environment:

- Trust and respect: Leaders build trust through transparency, honesty and respect in their interactions with team members. It also promotes a culture of respect among team members. - Recognition and reward: Recognizing and rewarding employees for their performance and contributions creates a positive work

environment and motivates people to do their best work.
-

 Work-life balance: Promoting a healthy work-life balance by providing flexible work arrangements and encouraging employees to take care of their own well-being can increase job satisfaction and productivity. - Employee Development: Leaders support the growth and development of team members by providing training, mentoring and career opportunities.

3. Hire the right people and build a high-performing team.

- Clearly define roles and expectations: Before hiring, leaders should clearly define the roles and responsibilities associated with each position and communicate expectations to potential candidates.

Competency-based hiring: Leaders should evaluate candidates based on skills, experience and cultural fit. Conducting interviews and reference checks will help identify the most suitable candidates.

- Diversity and Inclusion: Building a diverse and inclusive team provides diverse perspectives and encourages innovation. Leaders must actively promote diversity in hiring practices. - Encouraging collaboration: Leaders foster an environment that encourages collaboration and teamwork, allowing individuals to leverage each other's strengths and work toward a common goal.

 - Encourage continuous learning: Leaders should foster a culture of learning within their team, encouraging continuous skill development and knowledge sharing.

4. Develop strong communication and collaboration skills:

- Active listening: Leaders must listen carefully to team members and understand their concerns, ideas and opinions. This helps build trust and ensure effective communication.

 - Clear and open communication: Leaders must communicate clearly, avoid ambiguity and provide regular updates to ensure everyone is well informed. We should also encourage open dialogue and resolve conflicts quickly.

 - Empathy and emotional intelligence: Understanding and empathizing with the feelings and perspectives of team members helps leaders build stronger relationships and resolve conflicts effectively.

- Collaboration tools and practices: Using digital collaboration tools and establishing effective teamwork practices can improve communication and productivity, especially for remote or distributed teams.

 - Constructive feedback: Leaders should provide regular feedback to help people improve their performance. They should focus on constructive criticism and guide development.

 By focusing on these aspects, leaders can effectively drive business success and develop highly motivated, high-performing teams. Continuous improvement in these areas contributes to a positive work environment, increased productivity and better organizational results.

CHAPTER 4

A customer-centric approach is a business strategy that puts customers at the center of all decisions and actions. It's about understanding and meeting customer needs and expectations to create exceptional experiences that drive customer loyalty and advocacy. This approach recognizes that satisfied and loyal customers are critical to long-term success and sustainable growth.

Here are the key aspects of our customer-centric approach:

1. Customer First: This means putting our customers' needs, wants and interests first in all aspects of our business. It's about developing a deep understanding of your audience, their pain points and motivations. 2. Create great customer experiences: It's important to provide great experiences throughout the customer journey. This includes delivering a high-quality product or service, providing personalized interactions, and providing a seamless experience across multiple touchpoints.

3. Building customer loyalty and sustaining: A customer-centric approach focuses on building long-term relationships with customers. By consistently delivering value and exceeding expectations, you build loyalty and convert customers into advocates who actively recommend your company to others.

4. Harness the power of feedback and continuous improvement: Encouraging and actively seeking customer feedback is essential to understanding your customers' needs and preferences. This feedback can be collected through surveys, reviews, social media or direct contact. By listening to our customers and using them to continuously improve our products, services

and processes, we can increase customer satisfaction and retention. Implementing a customer-centric approach requires aligning an organization's culture, processes and strategies with its customers.

This includes training and empowering employees to prioritize customer needs, investing in customer service and support, using technology to improve customer interactions, and regularly measuring and analyzing customer satisfaction metrics.

Overall, our customer-centric approach aims to build strong and loyal customer relationships by consistently delivering outstanding experiences and continuously improving based on customer feedback. By putting your customers at the heart of your business, you can differentiate yourself from your competitors and create a sustainable competitive advantage.

CHAPTER 5

Develop a strong brand identity and positioning:

1. Define your brand: Be clear about what your brand stands for, its core values, mission and unique selling proposition (USP). Understand your target audience and their needs.

2. Brand Positioning: Define how you want your brand

to be perceived in the market. Define your competitive advantage and stand out from the competition.

3. Brand Message: Create a strong, consistent message that resonates with your target audience. Clearly and effectively communicate the benefits of your product or service.

Implement effective marketing strategies to maximize reach:

1. Market Research: Conduct thorough market research to understand your target audience, preferences,

behaviors and demographics. Identify market trends and opportunities.

2. Segmentation and Targeting: Segment your target audience based on characteristics such as age, location, interests and purchasing behavior. Tailor your marketing efforts to each segment.

3. Integrated Marketing Campaigns: Create comprehensive marketing campaigns using multiple channels and tactics, including advertising, public relations, content marketing and events. Be consistent across all channels.

4. Influencer Marketing: Work with influencers and thought leaders in your industry who have a large following and trust. It helps you reinforce your brand message and reach a wider audience.

5. Partnerships and collaborations: Identify potential partners or complementary brands to collaborate on joint marketing initiatives. This can help you increase your reach and attract new customers. Use of digital marketing channels and social networks:

1. Website Optimization: Create a user-friendly and visually-friendly website that reflects your brand and

provides a seamless browsing experience. Optimize for search engines (SEO) to improve organic visibility.

2. Content Marketing: Create relevant, high-quality content such as blog posts, videos, infographics, and guides that add value to your target audience. Share this content through your website, blog and social media.

3. Social Media Marketing: Make sure your target audience is on an active social media platform. Create compelling content, engage with your subscribers, run targeted ads, and leverage social media influencers.

4. Email Marketing: Build an email list and send periodic newsletters or promotional emails to strengthen customer relationships, share updates and increase sales. Customize emails based on customer preferences and behavior.

5. Paid Advertising: Increase brand visibility, generate traffic and generate leads using paid advertising channels such as Google Ads, social media advertising and display advertising. Set specific goals and track ad performance.

Measuring marketing effectiveness and adjusting strategies:

1. Set Measurable Goals: Define specific, measurable, achievable, relevant and time-bound (SMART) goals for your marketing efforts. These may include metrics such as website traffic, conversion rate, social media engagement and sales revenue.

2. Data Analytics: Track and analyze the performance of your marketing campaigns using analytics tools. Track key metrics, identify trends and gain insight into customer behavior and preferences.

3. A/B Testing: Experiment with different marketing strategies, messages, designs, and channels to find out what works best for your customers. Optimize your

results by testing variations on landing pages, emails, ads, and calls-to-action.

4. Customer Feedback: Solicit customer feedback through surveys, reviews and social media. Listen to them, address their concerns and incorporate their suggestions into your marketing strategy.

5. Continuous improvement: We regularly review and evaluate our marketing activities. Identify areas for improvement, adjust your strategy accordingly, and stay on top of industry trends and changes in consumer behavior.

CHAPTER 6

There are several key strategies and actions you can take to achieve increased sales and profits. Let's take a closer look at each aspect.

1. Build a strong sales pipeline:

- Identify and Identify Target Markets: Clearly define your ideal customer profile and identify the market segments that offer the greatest potential for your products and services - Lead Generation: Attract potential customers by implementing various lead generation strategies , including content marketing, social media marketing, search engine optimization and targeted advertising.

- Lead Qualification: Develop a lead qualification process to prioritize and focus on leads that can become paying customers. - Build Relationships: Build and maintain strong relationships with potential customers through personalized communication, follow-up and regular engagement.

- Use CRM software: Implement a customer relationship management (CRM) system to track and manage customers, develop relationships and streamline the sales process.

2. Effective sales and negotiation skills:

- Understand your customer's needs: Take the time to understand your customer's challenges, challenges and goals. Tailor your sales volume and solutions to meet your specific needs. - Value Proposition: Clearly describe the unique value and benefits that your products and services offer to your customers. Point out how your suggestion could solve their problem or improve their situation.

- Active listening: Learn to listen actively to understand your customers' concerns and objections. Solve these problems with well-crafted answers that show the value you add. - Building trust and relationships: Develop strong customer relationships based on trust, reliability and dependability. Show genuine interest in their development and be responsive to their needs. - Continuing education: Invest in training and development programs to improve your sales force's skills in effective communication, complaint handling and negotiation skills.

3. Develop strategic partnerships and collaborations:

- Identify complementary companies: Look for companies that offer your product or service but are not direct competitors. Look for partnerships where both parties can share resources, customer base or market access.

- Co-marketing efforts: Explore co-marketing initiatives with partners, such as co-branding campaigns, cross-promotion or referral programs. This will help you expand your reach and attract new customers.

- Value-added services: Consider partnering with other companies to provide value-added services to create bundled products or end-to-end solutions that provide more value to your customers.

4. Maximize revenue growth through innovation and diversification:

- Product/service innovation: continuous investment in research and development to improve existing products or develop new products/services in response to new customer needs or market trends.

 - Market Expansion: Explore new geographic markets or customer segments that align with your business goals. This may mean adapting your product or service to the specific needs of these new markets. -

Diversification: identify opportunities to expand product/service offerings into related or new industries. This diversification helps reduce risk and opens up additional income streams. - Customer feedback and iterations: We continuously seek customer feedback to identify areas for improvement or new features. Include this insight in your innovation and diversification strategy.

Keep in mind that consistent measurement and analysis of key sales and profit metrics is critical to monitoring progress and making data-driven decisions. Strategies are regularly reviewed and refined based on market dynamics, customer feedback and changing business needs.

CHAPTER 7

Financial management plays an important role in the success of a company. By implementing important financial management practices, businesses can increase profitability and achieve financial stability. Some important aspects to consider are:

1. Budgeting: Budgeting involves planning and

allocating financial resources to different parts of the business. It helps you set financial goals, manage costs and monitor performance. By preparing detailed budgets, companies can effectively manage their costs and revenue streams.

2. Forecasting: Forecasting is the prediction of future financial performance based on historical data and market trends. It helps companies make informed decisions by anticipating potential risks and opportunities. Accurate forecasting allows companies to prepare for contingencies and adjust their strategies accordingly.

3. Financial analysis: Regular financial analysis helps to assess the financial health of a company. This includes reviewing financial statements, reports and key performance indicators (KPIs). Financial analysis helps you identify areas for improvement, identify cost-effectiveness drivers, and make informed decisions about resource allocation.

4. Cash flow management: Cash flow management is essential for maintaining liquidity and meeting financial obligations. This includes controlling cash inflows and outflows, managing working capital and optimizing the timing of payments and collections. Effective cash flow

management ensures that the company has sufficient liquidity to cover expenses and invest in growth opportunities.

5. Working Capital Management: Working capital refers to the resources required for day-to-day operations. Effective working capital management includes optimizing inventory levels, managing receivables and payables, and reducing excess cash in a business. Businesses can improve cash flow and profitability by maintaining optimal levels of working capital.

6. Increase profitability: Businesses can increase

profitability by focusing on increasing revenue, controlling costs and improving efficiency. This can include strategies such as increasing the customer base, increasing prices, reducing wasteful spending, streamlining processes and leveraging technology. Regular monitoring of profitability parameters and identification of areas for improvement are essential for sustainable financial success.

7. Financial Stability: Financial stability means maintaining a strong financial position over the long term. This includes risk management, diversifying revenue streams and ensuring that the company can withstand economic fluctuations.

implementing good financial management practices, companies can build resilience and adapt to changing market conditions. It is important to note that financial management practices may vary by industry, company size and specific circumstances. Seeking expert advice from an accountant, financial advisor or consultant can provide valuable information tailored to your business needs.

CHAPTER 8

Personal development and well-being are important aspects of a fulfilling and balanced life. Here are some strategies and tips for each of the areas mentioned.

1. Balance between life and profession:

- Set boundaries: Set clear boundaries between work and personal life. Set certain working hours and try to separate yourself from work in your personal time.

- Prioritize activities: prioritize and allocate appropriate time. Make time for family, hobbies, relaxation and self-care.

- Delegation and outsourcing: Learn how to delegate tasks at work and at home to reduce your workload. If possible, consider outsourcing certain responsibilities.

- Mindfulness Training: Being fully present in every moment. When you work, focus on your work. When you are with your loved ones, be there and stay with them.

2. Building resilience and managing stress:

- Develop a support system: Surround yourself with positive and supportive people who can provide emotional support during difficult times.

- Practice self-care: Engage in activities that promote relaxation and rejuvenation. This could be exercise, meditation, journaling, or time in nature.

- Develop problem-solving skills: Learn effective problem-solving skills to overcome problems. Break complex problems into small, manageable steps.

- Maintain a positive mindset: develop a positive attitude and focus on your strengths. Be grateful and find meaning in difficult situations.

3. Continuous learning and self-improvement:

- Goal Setting: Set specific goals for personal growth and development. Break it down into smaller steps and create an action plan to achieve them.

- Reading and research: Read books, articles or listen to podcasts on topics that interest you. Expand your knowledge by attending workshops, seminars or taking online courses. -

Seek feedback: Accept constructive feedback from others and use it to identify areas for improvement. Always look back on your experiences and learn from your successes and failures.

- Accept the challenge: get out of your comfort zone and take on new challenges. It promotes personal growth and helps you gain new skills and knowledge.

4. Prioritize your physical and mental well-being.

- Regular physical exercise: Engage in your favorite physical activity. Follow a combination of cardio, strength training and flexibility training.

 - Get plenty of rest: prioritize sleep and maintain a consistent sleep pattern. Aim for 7-9 hours of quality sleep per night.

 - Learn stress management skills: explore stress reduction techniques such as deep breathing, mindfulness meditation or yoga. Find the one that suits you best.

- Seek professional help: If you are struggling with mental health, do not hesitate to contact a mental health professional. They can provide guidance and support.

Remember, personal development is a lifelong journey. It's important to be patient with yourself and celebrate the small victories along the way. To maintain a healthy balance in your life, review your priorities regularly and adjust as needed.

CHAPTER 9

Adaptation and innovation are essential for organizations to thrive in a rapidly changing business environment. Here are some key points for navigating change, driving innovation, identifying emerging trends, and implementing an agile strategy to grow your business.

One. Exploring Change and Embracing Classification:

- Adopt a growth mindset: foster a culture where employees are open to change and see challenges as opportunities for growth.

- Continuous training and development: Invest in training programs to equip employees with the necessary skills and knowledge to adapt to new technologies and market trends.

- Effective communication: clearly communicate the reason for the change and provide support to help your staff during the transition.

- Agility in decision-making: encourages decentralized decision-making and allows teams to quickly adapt and respond to changing circumstances.

2. Education for innovation and creativity:

- Encourage idea generation: Create a culture that values innovation by creating platforms and channels for employees to share their ideas. -

Support risk-taking:

Create a safe environment where employees feel comfortable taking calculated risks and experimenting in new ways.

- Collaboration and diversity: fostering cross-departmental collaboration and fostering creativity and innovation by embracing different perspectives.

 - Recognition and reward for innovation: Introduce a system of recognition and reward for the innovative contributions of employees.

3. Identify new trends and opportunities:

- Market research and analysis: Keep up with industry trends, customer needs and technological advances through market research and analysis. - External Partnerships:

Work with external partners such as startups, research institutes or industry experts to gain insights and access new technologies.

- Customer feedback and interaction: We actively seek customer feedback to understand changing needs and preferences.

- Internal Innovation Hubs: Establish specialized teams or departments focused on scanning the external environment and identifying new trends and opportunities.

4. Implement an agile strategy to grow your business:

- Agile project management: increase flexibility, improve collaboration and accelerate project delivery using an agile methodology such as Scrum or Kanban.

- Rapid prototyping: accommodate failed ideas by quickly creating prototypes or minimum viable products to test and validate ideas before implementing them at full scale.

- Data-driven decision-making: Uses data analytics to

understand customer behavior, market trends and performance metrics to enable informed decision-making.

- Flexible organizational structure: Implement a flexible organizational structure that facilitates rapid decision-making, promotes interoperability between functions and supports innovation.

By actively embracing change, fostering a culture of innovation, identifying emerging trends and implementing agile strategies, organizations can position themselves for growth and success in today's dynamic business environment.

CHAPTER 10

Long-term sustainable business strategy:

1. Adopt a sustainable business model: Incorporate sustainable practices into operations, such as reducing waste, conserving energy and promoting social and environmental responsibility. This not only helps protect the environment, but also improves your brand image and attracts environmentally conscious customers

2. Embrace innovation and adaptation: Stay ahead of industry trends and be open to

No innovation. Continually develop your products, services and processes to meet changing customer needs and market conditions. The use of technology increases operational efficiency and provides a competitive advantage.

3. Build strong relationships: Build long-term relationships with customers, suppliers and stakeholders. Provide excellent customer service, communicate effectively and respond to customer needs. Building trust and loyalty helps companies overcome difficulties and maintain stability.

4. Diversify your sources of income: Relying on a single

product or service can be risky. Look for opportunities to diversify products and revenue streams. This could include expanding into new markets, launching additional products or exploring strategic partnerships.

5. Invest in employee talent and development: Employees play an important role in the long-term success of our business. Invest in development through training programs, mentoring and advancement opportunities. A happy and skilled workforce translates into higher productivity and better customer service.

Business continuity and expansion plans:

1. Succession Planning: Develop a comprehensive succession plan to ensure a smooth transition in leadership and management when key personnel retire, leave or face unforeseen circumstances. Identify and nurture potential successors, provide them with the necessary training and exposure, and gradually assign them responsibility.

2. Establish a growth strategy: Define the company's growth goals and develop a strategic plan to achieve them. Research the market, identify opportunities for expansion, and identify the resources needed to support growth. This may include entering a new market,

launching a new product, or acquiring additional companies.

3. Secure funding: Assess funding needs for expansion and identify appropriate funding sources. This may include finding bank loans, attracting investors, or researching government grants and incentives. Create a strong business case and financial forecast to demonstrate the potential return on investment.

4. Strengthen your operational infrastructure: As you expand, ensure that your operational infrastructure can support growing demand. Evaluate systems, processes and technology to identify areas for improvement or

scalability. This allows companies to effectively manage growth and keep customers happy. Giving back to society and making a positive impact:

1. CSR (Corporate Social Responsibility): Establish a CSR strategy in line with the company's values and goals. Identify social or environmental issues that stakeholders can relate to and find ways to make a positive contribution. This may include supporting local charities, sponsoring community events or implementing sustainable practices in your business.

2. Volunteerism and employee involvement: Encourage employees to participate in volunteer activities and

support charities of interest. Offer paid volunteer hours, organize group volunteer events or start employee-led initiatives. Engaged employees who feel connected to their communities are happier and more productive.

3. Working with non-profit or non-governmental organizations: Working with reputable non-profit or non-governmental organizations (NGOs) to address social or environmental issues. This partnership allows inequalities is essential for social cohesion and sustainable economic

CHAPTER 11

Its importance to the state of the economy and society cannot be underestimated. The economy is the backbone of any society, influencing the well-being and livelihoods of individuals, businesses and governments. It includes various factors such as production, consumption, investment, employment and trade. It discusses the importance of the economy, acknowledges the challenges and highlights the need for effective revitalization solutions and objectives. Economic importance:

1. Employment and income: A strong economy provides jobs, reduces unemployment and generates income for individuals and households. This enables people to

become self-sufficient, meet their basic needs and improve their quality of life.

2. Living Standards: A thriving economy promotes higher living standards by stimulating economic growth and increasing productivity. It enables the production and availability of goods and services to improve the general well-being of people.

3. Government revenue: A healthy economy generates tax revenue that allows governments to fund public services such as education, health, infrastructure and social programs.

4. Business environment: A stable economy creates favorable conditions for business development. It encourages investment, innovation and entrepreneurship to improve productivity, competitiveness and economic diversification.

5. Sustainability and social inclusion: A sustainable economy promotes social inclusion by reducing poverty, inequality and social insecurity. This gives potential customers a sense of security and confidence. Challenges and needs for effective solutions:

1. Economic Inequality: Rising income inequality is a

major problem. It hinders social mobility, increases social segregation and undermines the general well-being of society. Effective solutions require policies that promote equitable distribution of wealth, access to quality education and employment for all.

2. Unemployment and Unemployment: Technological advances and economic changes can lead to job losses and unemployment. Addressing this challenge requires investing in education and retraining programs, supporting entrepreneurship and promoting dynamic labor markets.

3. Environmental sustainability: The impact of the

economy on the environment is a pressing issue. Balancing economic growth with environmental sustainability requires a shift to green technologies, the promotion of renewable energy sources and the adoption of sustainable production and consumption practices.

4. Globalization and Trade: The interconnectedness of economies creates problems such as unfair trade practices, protectionism and global economic instability. Effective solutions include promoting fair trade, developing international cooperation and diversifying the domestic economy.

5. Technological Advances: Rapid technological advances can disrupt traditional industries and create new economic opportunities. Preparing the workforce for the jobs of the future, promoting digital literacy and encouraging innovation are key to solving this problem.

The task of economic revitalization

1. Sustainable economic growth: promote long-term sustainable economic growth that balances economic, social and environmental objectives. This includes investment in infrastructure, research and development and encouraging innovation.

2. Job creation and skills development: Focus on job creation, especially in emerging sectors, by providing adequate training and skills training to ensure a capable workforce.

3. Inclusive growth: implement policies that reduce economic inequality, increase social mobility and share the benefits of economic

growth fairly across society.

4. Diversification of the economy:

Diversification of the economy to reduce dependence on one industry or sector. This includes supporting the growth of new industries, encouraging entrepreneurship and attracting investment in various industries.

5. Global Cooperation: Develop international cooperation and collaboration to address global economic challenges, promote fair trade practices, and enhance economic stability. Economic health is important to society and affects individuals, businesses and governments.

Recognizing the challenges you face and implementing effective solutions is critical to boosting the economy. By setting goals such as sustainable growth, job

creation, inclusive development and economic
diversification,

CHAPTER 12

Overview of different economic systems:

1. Capitalism: In a capitalist economic system, the
means of production are privately owned and individuals
and businesses operate in a competitive market.
Capitalism emphasizes the pursuit of individual
interests and the maximization of profits. Prices are

determined by supply and demand, and resource allocation is largely determined by market force.s.

2. Socialism: Socialism advocates collective or national ownership of the means of production. The goal is to increase social security and reduce income inequality. In a socialist system, the government plays an important role in allocating resources and redistributing wealth. Prices can be regulated and are often focused on the public supply of goods and services.

3. Mixed Economy: A mixed economy combines elements of capitalism and socialism. In them there is a mixture of private and public ownership of the means of

production. Governments intervene in the economy in a variety of ways, including regulation, subsidies, and social protection. Most modern economies are mixed economies with varying degrees of government involvement. Strengths and weaknesses of each system:

1. Capitalism:

- Strengths: Capitalism encourages innovation and entrepreneurship, promotes individual freedom and choice, and promotes efficiency and productivity. This can lead to economic growth and wealth creation. It allows for a wider range of consumer goods and services and promotes competition that improves quality and lowers prices.

- Weaknesses: Capitalism can lead to income inequality and the concentration of wealth, because the richer you already are, the greater your chances of economic success. Market failures such as externalities (e.g. pollution) and undersupply of public goods may occur. Capitalism can also lead to boom and bust cycles, economic instability and financial crises.

2. socialism:

- Strengths: Socialism aims to reduce income inequality and ensure a more equitable distribution of resources. We can ensure that all members of society have access to basic needs such as health care and education.

Socialism can also lead to social cohesion and cooperation. -

Weaknesses: As the profit motive declines, socialism can encourage innovation and entrepreneurship. Centralized decision-making and lack of competition in the market can lead to inefficiency and misallocation of resources. Without proper checks and balances, socialism can lead to excessive government intervention and a lack of individual freedom.

3. Mixed economy:

- Strengths: A mixed economy combines the strengths of capitalism and socialism. They find a balance between personal freedom and social welfare. State intervention can eliminate market failures, provide public goods, and reduce income inequality. Mixed economies often have strong social safety nets and can promote economic stability and growth.

- Weaknesses: A mixed economy can struggle to find the right balance between market forces and government intervention. There may be disagreements about the scope and effectiveness of government programs and regulations. In some cases, mixed economies may still face income inequality and unequal access to opportunities. Assess the current economic system and determine the direction for improvement:

An assessment of the current economic system depends on the specific country and special conditions. However, in most economies, some common areas for improvement include:

1. Income Inequality: Tackling the Growing Wealth Gap and Sharing the Benefits of Economic Growth More Equitably.

2. Sustainability: Transition to more sustainable and greener economic models, taking into account climate

change and resource depletion. Three. Social Security: Strengthening social safety nets, health and education systems to ensure access and opportunities for all members of society. 4. Innovation and productivity: increasing investment in entrepreneurship, research and development and human capital to drive long-term economic growth.

5. Regulation and Supervision: Ensure effective regulation and supervision to prevent financial market failures.

CHAPTER 13

Determining important economic issues requires a comprehensive analysis of various factors and their interrelationships. Here are some steps to help you identify and prioritize economic problems.

1. Data Research and Analysis: We collect relevant data and research on economic indicators such as GDP growth rate, unemployment rate, inflation rate, income distribution, poverty level and other relevant economic indicators. It provides a starting point for understanding the current economic situation.

2. Identify root causes: Investigate major factors contributing to economic problems. Unemployment, for

example, can be caused by a variety of factors, such as technological advances, skills shortages, job shortages, or economic downturns. Inflation can be caused by factors such as excessive money supply, supply chain disruptions, or energy price fluctuations. Income inequality can arise from differences in access to education, technological advances, tax policy, or market concentration. Understanding the root cause is essential to developing effective strategies to address these issues.

3. Interdependence analysis: Economic problems are often interconnected, and solving one can affect the others. Reducing income inequality requires addressing

issues such as education, labor market reform or fiscal policy. By analyzing interdependencies, decision makers can determine the most effective and holistic approach to addressing multiple issues simultaneously.

4. Consider short-term and long-term consequences: Some economic problems may have immediate consequences that require immediate resolution, while others may have long-term consequences that require strategic planning. It is necessary to assess the importance and relevance of impacts on society and the economy in order to prioritize the most pressing issues.

5. Stakeholder engagement: Seek input from a variety

of stakeholders, such as economists, politicians, business leaders, union representatives, academics and citizens. Their insights can provide valuable insights and help identify issues that are important to different sectors of society.

6. Evaluate policy options: Consider different policy interventions and their potential effectiveness in addressing the identified economic challenges. This assessment should consider the feasibility, cost-effectiveness and potential unintended consequences of each policy option.

7. Prioritize by impact and feasibility: Assess the

potential impact of solving each economic problem and compare it to the feasibility of implementing the desired policy. Prioritize issues that have the greatest potential for positive change and are achievable in the current economic and political context. It is important to note that economic issues may vary by country and region, and prioritization processes should be tailored to specific circumstances. Economic conditions change over time, requiring constant monitoring and reassessment.

CHAPTER 14

Fiscal policy is the use of government spending and

taxes to influence the economy. It plays an important role in promoting economic stability and stimulating economic growth. Here are some key considerations regarding the role of fiscal policy in stabilizing and growing the economy, the effectiveness of government intervention, and strategies for using fiscal policy to achieve specific economic goals.

1. Economic stability and economic growth:

- Fiscal policy aims to stabilize the economy in periods of recession or inflation. It can be expanded or contracted according to economic conditions.

- During a recession, expansionary fiscal policy increases government spending and cuts taxes to increase aggregate demand, increase economic activity, and reduce unemployment. - In times of inflation, fiscal tightening aims to reduce government spending and raise taxes to cool aggregate demand, limit inflationary pressures, and maintain price stability.

- Fiscal policy can target long-term growth through investments in infrastructure, education and research and development that can increase productivity and increase economic competitiveness.

2. Effects of state intervention:

- The effectiveness of fiscal policy depends on many factors, including current economic conditions, the size and timing of policy actions, and the response of individuals and businesses to changes in taxes and government spending.

 - To implement fiscal policy, economic conditions must be carefully reviewed and policies must be monitored and adjusted to produce desirable results

. - The effectiveness of fiscal policy can be influenced by

factors such as leakages (e.g. income instead of savings or spending) and accumulation effects (e.g. high interest rates and reduced private investment due to high public debt).

3. Strategies to stimulate economic growth, reduce unemployment and control inflation:

- Stimulating economic growth: expansionary fiscal policy can be used to stimulate economic growth by increasing government spending on infrastructure projects, providing tax breaks to businesses, and investing in human capital through education and training programs. These actions can increase aggregate demand, increase investment and productivity, and contribute to long-term economic growth.

- Reducing unemployment: Fiscal policy can be used to encourage job creation during periods of high unemployment. This can be done by increasing government spending on labor-intensive projects, providing subsidies or incentives to businesses to hire more workers, and implementing training and retraining programs to improve workers' skills. - Inflation control:

Tight fiscal policy can be used when inflationary pressures arise. The package includes a combination of the two to help reduce government spending, raise taxes or reduce demand, control inflation, and maintain price stability. It is important to note that fiscal policy interacts with other economic policies, such as monetary policy and structural reforms. Co-ordinated and coherent policy actions are often required to effectively achieve the desired economic outcomes. In addition, the effectiveness of fiscal policy may vary with economic conditions, so policymakers must carefully assess specific circumstances and adjust their strategies accordingly.

CHAPTER 15

Central banks play an important role in managing the economy by implementing monetary policy. They are responsible for maintaining price stability, promoting full employment and ensuring the stability of the financial system. The main functions of central banks in economic management are:

1. Inflation Control: The central bank aims to maintain price stability by keeping inflation within a target range. They use a variety of monetary policy tools to control the money supply, influence interest rates, and control inflationary pressures.

2. Conducting monetary policy: Central banks use monetary policy to regulate the money supply and influence interest rates. Adjusting these variables can

affect overall economic activity by influencing credit costs, spending patterns, and investment decisions.

3. Control of the money supply: Central banks have the ability to control the money supply in the economy. They do this using tools such as open market operations (buying and selling government securities), regulating bank reserve requirements, and discount rates (the rate at which banks borrow money from central banks).

4. Lender of last resort: Central banks act as lenders of last resort to provide liquidity to commercial banks and other financial institutions during financial crises. This helps stabilize the financial system and prevent bank

failure or system collapse. 5. Supervision and regulation of banks: Central banks often have supervisory and regulatory powers over banks and financial institutions. They establish and enforce prudential regulations to ensure the stability and soundness of the banking system.

Let us now discuss the tools and methods of monetary policy.

1. Open Market Operations (OMO): This involves the buying and selling of government securities (bonds) in the open market. Central banks inject money into the economy by buying bonds, increasing the money supply. Conversely, selling bonds reduces the money supply.

The OMO is the most widely used tool for conducting monetary policy.

2. Reserve requirement: The central bank sets a reserve requirement, which determines how much a bank must hold as a deposit reserve. By regulating these requirements, central banks can influence the amount banks can lend and the money supply.

3. Discount Rate: The discount rate is the rate at which banks can borrow directly from the central bank. By changing this ratio, the central bank can affect the bank's borrowing costs, which affects interest rates for businesses and individuals.

4. Interest rate policy: Central banks use interest rate policy to influence the cost of borrowing in the economy. By adjusting policy rates, such as the benchmark rate or the federal funds rate, central banks affect lending rates, which in turn affect consumer spending, investment, and economic growth.

The relationship between interest rates, money supply and economic indicators is complex and interconnected.

1. Impact on borrowing costs: Low interest rates reduce borrowing costs, encouraging businesses and individuals to borrow for investment and consumption. This increase in borrowing and spending could boost economic growth. Conversely, high interest rates raise

the cost of borrowing, which dampens borrowing and reduces economic activity.

2. Money supply and inflation: Central banks control the money supply, and changes in the money supply can affect inflation. A rapid increase in the money supply without an increase in the production of goods and services can create inflationary pressures. By regulating the money supply, central banks can influence the rate of inflation.

3.Economic Indicators: The overall state of the economy, including factors such as GDP growth, employment levels, and price stability, affects the effectiveness of monetary policy. By controlling interest rates and the money supply, central banks aim to stabilize the economy and maintain stable growth and stable price levels. Monetary policy is only one aspect of general economic management and is closely related to fiscal policy (government spending and tax decisions).

CHAPTER 16

Encouraging innovation and entrepreneurship is key to boosting economic growth and fostering dynamic and prosperous societies. Here are some key points to remember when implementing strategies to highlight the role of innovation, identify barriers and develop an entrepreneurial and innovative culture.

1: The role of innovation in stimulating economic growth:

Innovation plays an important role in economic growth by creating new industries, improving productivity and strengthening competitiveness. This leads to the development of new products, services and business models that stimulate demand, create jobs and create wealth. By encouraging innovation, countries can strengthen their economies and improve the living standards of their citizens.

2. Identify barriers to innovation and entrepreneurship:

A variety of obstacles can stand in the way of innovation and entrepreneurship. These include:

all. Lack of access to capital: Limited access to finance can be a major barrier, especially for entrepreneurs with innovative ideas. Governments and financial institutions can play a role by providing funding options such as grants, loans and venture capital, especially for start-ups and innovative companies.

B. Regulatory Pressures: Complex and stringent regulations can stifle innovation and entrepreneurship. Governments must work to create a regulatory environment that encourages innovation while providing the necessary safeguards. This may include streamlining regulations, reducing bureaucratic barriers and implementing supportive policies

C. Risk Aversion and Fear of Failure: A culture of risk aversion can hinder entrepreneurial endeavors. Education and awareness programs should focus on changing mindsets and developing a culture that embraces calculated risk, learns from failure, and rewards innovation.

d. Limited access to networks and resources:

A :lack of networks and resources can hinder an entrepreneur's ability to access mentors, partners and market opportunities. Creating incubators, accelerators and innovation centers can provide startups and entrepreneurs with valuable resources, networking platforms and guidance.

E. Inadequate Education and Training: Lack of adequate education and training in innovation and entrepreneurship can limit an individual's ability to engage in entrepreneurship. Integrating entrepreneurship education into school curricula, offering special programs and encouraging

collaboration between academia and industry can help
overcome these barriers.

3. Strategies for innovation and the development of
corporate culture:

Governments, companies and communities can
implement a variety of strategies to promote innovation
and entrepreneurship.

A. Encouraging collaboration and knowledge sharing: To
encourage and promote a supportive ecosystem for
education by encouraging collaboration between
business, academia and research institutions. Initiatives

such as innovation challenges, hackathons and open innovation platforms can bring different perspectives together.

. Start-up support and resource provision:

Create start-up-friendly policies such as tax breaks, subsidies and start-up support grants. We develop incubators, accelerators and co-working spaces to provide mentorship, infrastructure and network access to startups. Public-private partnerships can play an important role in supporting startups.

Seed. Encouraging entrepreneurship education: Introduce entrepreneurship education programs that emphasize practical skills, creativity and problem solving at all levels of education. We promote entrepreneurship as a viable career option and offer educational programs to enhance entrepreneurial spirit and mindset.

 D. Deregulation and Removing Barriers: Fix and simplify regulations that can hinder entrepreneurship and innovation. Introduce a regulatory framework that balances ease of doing business with necessary security measures.

Creating a fast and efficient mechanism for corporate registration and licensing processes. E. Encourage risk-taking and celebrate success: Recognize and celebrate successful entrepreneurs who inspire others. Foster a culture that embraces calculated risk-taking, learning from failure, rewarding innovation through awards, grants and public recognition.

F. Develop a supportive ecosystem: Develop networks and communities that facilitate collaboration, mentorship, and knowledge sharing among entrepreneurs. As a mentor and advisor for the development of start-ups, we encourage the participation of experienced entrepreneurs and investors. Stimulating innovation and entrepreneurship requires a comprehensive approach.

CHAPTER 17

Investment in human capital is essential for personal and social development. Recognizing the importance of developing knowledge and skills, improving access to quality education and training, closing skills gaps and promoting lifelong learning. Let's take a closer look at each of these aspects.

1. Recognize the importance of developing knowledge and skills:

Education plays an important role in shaping individuals and societies. Recognizing the importance of education, governments, businesses and individuals can prioritize their investments in this sector. Affordable and quality education gives people knowledge, critical thinking skills and a broader understanding of the world. It also promotes creativity, problem solving, and social skills that are important for personal growth and contribution to society.

2. Improving access to quality education and vocational training:

Increasing access to education means ensuring that everyone has the opportunity to receive a quality education, regardless of background or socio-economic status. This includes investing in infrastructure, providing grants and financial assistance, and removing barriers such as discrimination and inequality. Vocational training programs can also increase employment and economic growth by giving people the practical skills and knowledge needed for a particular industry or job.

3. Bridging the skills gap and promoting lifelong learning:

The skills required in the labor market are constantly evolving due to technological advances and the changing economic environment. It is essential to address skills gaps by adapting educational programs to the needs of the labor market. This includes promoting science, technology, engineering and mathematics (STEM) education and the development of important unusual skills such as communication, problem solving and adaptability.

We also need to encourage lifelong learning so that people can continuously update their skills throughout their careers. Adult education programs, professional development initiatives and online learning platforms can help with this. Encouraging lifelong learning enables people to remain relevant in the labor market, adapt to new skills and contribute to personal and professional growth. An investment in human capital is an investment in the future. By prioritizing education, skills

development and lifelong learning, society can drive
innovation, economic growth and social progress, while
giving people the tools they need to succeed in an ever-
changing world.

CHAPTER 18

International trade plays an important role in the
economic development of countries by promoting
specialization, increasing market access and
stimulating economic growth. However, there are also
some benefits and challenges to explore.

Trade agreements also have a significant impact on the

economy, and strategies to expand international trade and attract foreign investment are essential for countries seeking to strengthen economic integration. Let's take a closer look at each of the following topics.

1. Advantages and Disadvantages of International Trade:

A. Advantages:

- Economic growth: International trade allows countries to capitalize on their comparative advantage to increase output, employment and overall economic growth.

- Market Access: Trade provides access to a large

market, allowing businesses to expand their customer base and increase their profits.

 - Specialization and efficiency: Countries can focus on producing goods and services with comparative advantages that increase efficiency and productivity. -

Benefits for consumers: international trade increases consumer choice by providing access to a wider range of goods and services at competitive prices. - Technology transfer: Trade facilitates the transfer of technology and knowledge between countries and promotes innovation and technological progress.

B. The task:

- Job displacement: International trade can move workers into industries that are not globally competitive, causing unemployment and social problems

. - Trade imbalance: Countries can experience trade deficits or surpluses that can affect domestic industries, exchange rates and overall economic stability.

- Dependence: excessive dependence on imports for

daily necessities can lead to vulnerability and dependence on other countries. - Market Volatility: Global economic fluctuations, exchange rate fluctuations and changes in trade policies can create uncertainty and risk for companies involved in international trade. - Environmental impact: Increasing international trade can lead to environmental problems such as pollution, deforestation and transport-related carbon emissions.

2. Trade agreements and their impact on the economy:

Trade agreements are agreements negotiated between countries to facilitate trade by reducing barriers such as tariffs and quotas. These contracts can have significant economic impact, including:

- Market access: Trade agreements often increase market access for goods and services by eliminating or reducing tariff and non-tariff barriers.

- Economic integration: Trade agreements can facilitate closer economic integration by harmonizing rules, standards and investment rules between participating countries.

- Foreign Direct Investment (FDI):

Trade agreements can increase FDI flows by providing a more predictable and favorable investment environment by protecting intellectual property rights and investor dispute settlement mechanisms.

- Industry competitiveness: Trade agreements can increase the competitiveness of domestic industries by exposing them to international competition, stimulating innovation and productivity gains.

- Economic growth: by stimulating trade and investment flows, trade agreements contribute to overall economic growth and development.

Three. Strategies for expanding international trade and attracting foreign investment:

A. Trade Promotion:

- Diversification: Countries can reduce their dependence on more trading partners by opening new markets and expanding the range of exported goods and services.

- Market research: Market research helps identify potential export opportunities and understand consumer preferences and demand in the target market.

- Export promotion: Governments can provide incentives

and support programs for businesses to participate in international trade, such as export financing, trade missions and trade fairs.

- Trade facilitation: Streamlining customs procedures, reducing red tape and improving logistics and infrastructure can increase trade efficiency.

rain. Promotion of investments:

- Investor-friendly policies: The implementation of open and predictable investment policies, the protection of property rights and the guarantee of the rule of law attract foreign investors.

- Investment promotion: The government can offer tax breaks, subsidies and other incentives to attract foreign direct investment. - Infrastructure development: transport, communications,

CHAPTER 19

Sustainable development is a concept that seeks to meet the needs of the present without compromising the ability of future generations to meet their own needs. We recognize the interdependence of economic, social and environmental aspects of development and strive to find a balance between them. Fundamentally, sustainable development promotes the responsible use of resources, social inclusion and environmental protection. It recognizes that economic growth is necessary to improve people's lives, but emphasizes that this growth must be achieved in a way that minimizes negative impacts on the environment and society.

Green technologies and renewable energies play an important role in achieving sustainable development. Green technologies include a wide range of green practices and innovations that increase energy efficiency, reduce greenhouse gas emissions and minimize resource depletion. These technologies can include renewable energy sources such as solar, wind, hydro and geothermal energy, energy efficient buildings, sustainable transport systems and waste management solutions.

The advantage of renewable energy sources is that they are naturally replenished and have lower greenhouse gas emissions compared to fossil fuels. They help combat climate change, reduce air pollution and reduce dependence on finite and environmentally damaging resources.

Promoting green practices includes adopting sustainable behaviors and transitioning to a green economy. These changes include the integration of sustainable principles in various sectors, including agriculture, industry, transport and construction. This includes implementing policies and practices that prioritize resource efficiency, waste reduction and the use of clean technologies.

A green economy refers to an economic system that focuses on sustainable development, prioritizing low-carbon, resource-efficient and socially inclusive practices. This includes sectors that contribute to environmental protection and social welfare, such as renewable energy sources, ecotourism, organic farming and sustainable production.

The transition to a green economy requires governments, businesses and individuals to work together and implement a variety of strategies. This may include encouraging investment in renewable energy sources, promoting sustainable business practices through regulations and standards, investing in green research and development, supporting sustainable agricultural and forestry practices, and promoting sustainable education and awareness.

sustainable development encompasses the pursuit of economic growth, social cohesion and environmental protection. The transition to green technologies, renewable energies and a green economy is an integral part of achieving the Sustainable Development Goals. Adopting green practices and making sustainable decisions creates a more prosperous and sustainable future for future generations.

CHAPTER20

Assessing the importance of infrastructure for economic development:

Infrastructure plays an important role in stimulating economic development and ensuring long-term growth. These include transport networks (highways, railways, airports, ports), energy systems (energy generation, transport and distribution), telecommunications networks (internet, telecommunications), water and sanitation facilities and social infrastructure (schools, hospitals) .

1. Connectivity and mobility: Efficient transport systems reduce transaction costs, facilitate the movement of goods and people and improve market integration. It promotes trade, attracts investment and stimulates economic activity.

2. Productivity and competitiveness: A reliable energy and communications infrastructure enables businesses to operate efficiently, access markets and innovate. Increase productivity by reducing downtime, increasing

operational efficiency and improving communication with suppliers and customers.

3. Human capital development: Quality social infrastructure, such as education and healthcare, contributes to the development of a skilled workforce and a healthy population. This, in turn, increases labor productivity and attracts investment.

4. Regional development: Well-planned infrastructure projects can contribute to balanced regional development by connecting remote areas, creating new economic opportunities and reducing regional disparities.

Infrastructure project financing and implementation strategies:

Financing and implementing infrastructure projects can be complex and require significant investment. Here are some commonly used strategies.

1. Public financing: The government can finance infrastructure projects by allocating public funds from the budget. These include tax revenues, government loans and grants from international organizations or bilateral agreements.

2. Public-Private Partnership (PPP): PPP involves

collaboration between public authorities and private companies to develop, finance and manage infrastructure projects. The private sector provides capital, expertise and efficiency, while the government Hiprovides the regulatory framework and shares the risk.

3. Infrastructure Bonds: Governments can issue bonds specifically designed to finance infrastructure. These bonds are often long-term products with attractive interest rates that appeal to investors interested in fixed income.

4. Multilateral Development Banks (MDBs): MDBs, such

as the World Bank and Regional Development Banks, provide loans, grants, and technical assistance to support infrastructure projects in developing countries. They use their resources to attract private investment and ensure the viability of the project

. 5. Project financing: Providing financing based on the cash flow generated by the infrastructure project itself rather than the creditworthiness of the project sponsor. Lenders evaluate a project's earning potential and risks before providing financing.

Maximizing the impact of public investments on economic growth:

To maximize the impact of public investment on economic growth, it is important to consider the following strategies.

1. Prioritization and strategic planning: Governments should prioritize infrastructure development based on its potential to stimulate economic growth. Strategic planning ensures that resources are allocated efficiently and projects are aligned with wider development goals.

2. Effective project selection and management: Rigorous project selection criteria, feasibility studies and cost-benefit analysis are essential to identify projects with the greatest potential impact. Effective

project management ensures on-time execution, cost control and quality results.

3. Regulatory and institutional reform: Streamlining regulatory frameworks, improving governance structures and reducing bureaucratic barriers can increase the efficiency and transparency of infrastructure development. This will attract private investment, reduce project delays and reduce corruption risks.

4. Cooperation and coordination: Governments should promote cooperation between different levels of government, private sector stakeholders and

international organizations. Effective coordination improves project planning, resource allocation and knowledge sharing.

5. Monitoring and Evaluation: Regular monitoring and evaluation of infrastructure projects enables corrective action and ensures accountability. This helps to identify barriers, improve the implementation process and measure the real impact on economic growth. By using these strategies, countries can strengthen infrastructure, boost public investment and promote sustainable economic development.

CHAPTER 21

Social welfare and inclusive growth are key concepts to combat income and social inequality and promote fair societies. Here are some points related to these topics.

1. Eliminating income and social inequality:

- Progressive Taxation: Implementing a progressive taxation system helps redistribute wealth by taxing higher earners at a higher rate and using that revenue to support welfare programs.

 - Minimum Wage Law: Setting a minimum wage and gradually increasing it reduces the chances of workers earning a decent income and living in poverty.

- Access to quality education: ensuring equal educational opportunities, including access to quality schools, resources and scholarships, can help reduce educational disparities and improve social mobility.

- Job creation and fair labor practices: By encouraging job creation, promoting fair labor practices and supporting workers' rights, we can reduce income inequality and improve working conditions for all.

2. Promotion of inclusive growth policies

- Investment in infrastructure: Infrastructure development, such as transport networks, power grids and internet connectivity, contributes to economic growth and job creation, especially in vulnerable regions.

- Supporting small and medium-sized enterprises (SMEs): providing financial and technical assistance to small and medium-sized enterprises (SMEs) enables the development of entrepreneurship, job creation and local economic growth.

- Access to financial services: expanding access to banking services, microfinance and credit for disadvantaged groups can help them start businesses, invest and improve their livelihoods. - Regional development: regional disparities can be addressed by investing in economically vulnerable regions to promote balanced regional development and stimulate industries with growth potential.

3. Providing a social safety net and supporting the vulnerable

- Social assistance programs: Establishing and strengthening social assistance programs such as unemployment benefits, cash assistance, and food assistance can provide a safety net for individuals and families experiencing economic hardship. - Access to health care: ensuring universal access to affordable health services, including health insurance and primary care, protects vulnerable populations from the financial burden of health care costs.

- Support for children and families: by implementing policies such as child benefit, parental leave and affordable childcare, families can reduce their economic burden and support children's development.

- Support for the elderly and disabled: Support for the elderly and disabled to receive the necessary support and lead a dignified life through pension, disability benefits, long-term care, etc. Overall, an integrated approach to social welfare and inclusive growth involves a combination of progressive policies, targeted interventions and investments in human capital and infrastructure to reduce income inequality, promote inclusive economic growth and provide a safety net for vulnerable populations .

CHAPTER 22.

MOST POPULAR BUSINESSES

E-commerce and online retail are becoming increasingly important in the digital age. Here are some key points about the topic you mentioned.

¡ E-Transactions: Strategies for starting and growing a successful online store include creating a secure and easy-to-use payment gateway to facilitate e-transactions. This includes integrating popular payment methods such as credit cards, digital wallets and online banking. Implementing strong security measures is critical to protecting customer data and building trust.

2. Digital Marketing Techniques: To generate traffic, sales and growth in the online retail industry, businesses need to use a variety of digital marketing techniques. These include search engine optimization (SEO) to improve website visibility, pay-per-click (PPC) advertising to drive targeted traffic, social media

marketing to connect with customers, cultivate customers leads and generate repeat business. This includes email marketing for

3. Control the customer experience: Creating a seamless and personalized user experience is essential to building customer loyalty in the digital age. This includes optimizing the site design, navigation and product presentation to improve the overall shopping experience. Great customer service through live chat, chatbots and fast response times are also key to customer satisfaction.

4. Optimizing the Supply Chain: Optimizing the delivery

process is essential to meet the expectations of online shoppers. This includes optimizing inventory management, building efficient warehouses and fulfillment operations, and partnering with trusted logistics service providers. We offer a variety of shipping options such as express delivery or click and collect to enhance customer convenience.

5. Global reach in the digital age: Online retailers can reach a global customer base beyond local markets. With e-commerce, geographic boundaries are no longer limited, allowing businesses to target customers around the world. This requires adapting to international regulations, localizing websites for different languages

and cultures, and considering logistics and customs requirements for cross-border shipments. Successful e-commerce and online retail strategies typically succeed in digital markets by integrating technological advancements, marketing techniques, customer-centric approaches, and efficient logistics operations.

CHAPTER 23

1. Trusted advisors: Trusted advisors are experts who specialize in building and maintaining relationships based on trust with clients. They understand the importance of trust in business relationships and work to build trust and confidence. Trusted advisors use effective communication skills, active listening skills,

and empathy to connect with clients and build long-term partnerships. Their main goal is to help customers feel confident and secure in their business transactions, resulting in a successful outcome for both parties.

2. Research Tip: Research is an important aspect of any consulting or professional activity. Using the right tools, equipment and techniques is critical to research success. These may include market research tools, data analysis software, survey platforms and industry-specific resources. Researchers must also keep abreast of the latest trends, developments and best practices in their field to ensure the accuracy and reliability of their research results. Using effective research methods,

consultants can gather valuable information to support decision-making and make informed recommendations to clients.

3. Effective Communication Skills: In the consulting and professional services industries, effective communication plays an important role in building strong relationships with clients and influencing their decisions. Communication technologies refer to the tools, platforms and strategies used to ensure seamless and reliable communication. These may include email systems, video conferencing platforms, project management software, customer relationship management (CRM) systems, and collaboration tools. Using these technologies, consultants can communicate

effectively with clients, provide a rapid exchange of information, and communicate their expertise in a persuasive and impactful manner.

4. Strategic Consulting: Strategic consulting helps companies develop and implement effective strategies to achieve their goals. Strategy consultants analyze a company's current situation, market dynamics and competitive landscape to identify opportunities and challenges. It then creates a strategic plan and provides actionable recommendations to improve performance, drive growth and gain a competitive advantage. Strategy consultants work closely with clients' leadership teams to guide them through the planning,

implementation and evaluation phases of strategic initiatives.

5. Business Model Management Consulting: Business Model Management Consulting focuses on the effective management and execution of consulting projects. It covers several aspects, including project scope, resource allocation, scheduling and quality assurance. Business model management consultants ensure that projects are well organized, deliver results and exceed client expectations. Streamline processes and improve project outcomes using project management methodologies such as Agile or Waterfall. By effectively

managing the consulting business model, consultants can maximize project success and client satisfaction.

The food and beverage industry - a diverse and dynamic industry that includes a wide range of businesses including restaurants, cafes, bars, food companies, etc. It plays an important role in the economy and gives people access to a wide variety of culinary experiences and products. Based on the sentences you have provided, let's look at some key points related to catering operations, business commissions and maintenance in the food industry, strategic menu engineering and the concept of the Farmer's Table.

1. Restaurant success: more than just an opening

concept

In the highly competitive food service industry, opening a variety of concepts is a remarkable achievement. This demonstrates the restaurant's ability to successfully create and execute a variety of dining experiences or cuisines with multiple brand identities. This success reflects diversity, innovation and understanding of different consumer preferences. Opening more concepts can help restaurants reach more customers and increase their market share.

2. Hobers Entrepreneuriat: Commissions and maintenance for food companies

"Hobers Entrepreneuriat" seems to refer to specific companies or organizations that order and serve food businesses. In the food industry, entrepreneurs play an important role in building and maintaining a food business. We can help your food business thrive by providing services such as business consulting, financial assistance, marketing assistance and operational guidance. The start-up aspect may include helping new entrepreneurs start a food business, and maintenance may include ongoing support and optimization of an existing food business.

3. Engineering Menu: Strategic Design Menu

Menu engineering refers to the strategic design and composition of menus in a restaurant or cafe. This includes carefully manipulating menu layout, descriptions, pricing and item placement to influence customer behavior and increase profitability. Menu design techniques often consider factors such as item popularity, profitability, placement and use of design elements to focus on a particular item. The goal is to direct customers to high-margin products while enhancing the dining experience.

4. Boerentafel: Sustainable practices in the food industry

The farm-to-table concept emphasizes the use of farm-fresh, locally sourced ingredients in the food industry at large. The goal is to provide customers with a dining experience that reflects the quality and sustainability of local food. A farm-to-table concept may include working directly with local farmers and producers to feature their products on the menu.

This approach supports local agriculture, reduces our carbon footprint and appeals to consumers looking for fresh, healthy and eco-friendly dining options.

The sentences given are relatively short and the descriptions given without further context are general in nature.

CONCLUSION

The Business Success Blueprint" offers a roadmap to achieving lasting success in the dynamic and competitive world of business.ROY. T .LEWIS provides readers with invaluable insights, actionable tips, and real-world examples to inspire and guide entrepreneurs on their journey towards building thriving businesses. By implementing the strategies outlined in this book, readers will gain a competitive edge and increase their chances of creating a lasting impact in their respective industries.

www.ingramcontent.com/pod-product-compliance
Lightning Source LLC
Chambersburg PA
CBHW072029230526
45466CB00020B/1157